Facts About the Manta Ray

By Lisa Strattin

© 2019 Lisa Strattin

FREE BOOK

FREE FOR ALL SUBSCRIBERS

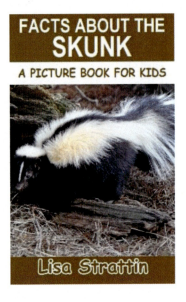

LisaStrattin.com/Subscribe-Here

BOX SET

- **FACTS ABOUT THE POISON DART FROGS**
- **FACTS ABOUT THE THREE TOED SLOTH**
  - **FACTS ABOUT THE RED PANDA**
  - **FACTS ABOUT THE SEAHORSE**
  - **FACTS ABOUT THE PLATYPUS**
  - **FACTS ABOUT THE REINDEER**
  - **FACTS ABOUT THE PANTHER**
- **FACTS ABOUT THE SIBERIAN HUSKY**

LisaStrattin.com/BookBundle

Facts for Kids Picture Books by Lisa Strattin

Little Blue Penguin, Vol 92

Chipmunk, Vol 5

Frilled Lizard, Vol 39

Blue and Gold Macaw, Vol 13

Poison Dart Frogs, Vol 50

Blue Tarantula, Vol 115

African Elephants, Vol 8

Amur Leopard, Vol 89

Sabre Tooth Tiger, Vol 167

Baboon, Vol 174

Sign Up for New Release Emails Here

LisaStrattin.com/subscribe-here

Some coloring pages might be of the general species due to lack of available images.

I have relied on my own observations as well as many different sources for this book and I have done my best to check facts and give credit where it is due. In the event that any material is used without proper permission, please contact me so that the oversight can be corrected.

Contents

INTRODUCTION...9

CHARACTERISTICS 11

APPEARANCE 13

REPRODUCTION...15

LIFE SPAN 17

SIZE 19

HABITAT..21

DIET 23

ENEMIES...25

SUITABILITY AS PETS...27

INTRODUCTION

The Manta Ray is a large species of flattened fish, closely related to other fish, like the shark.

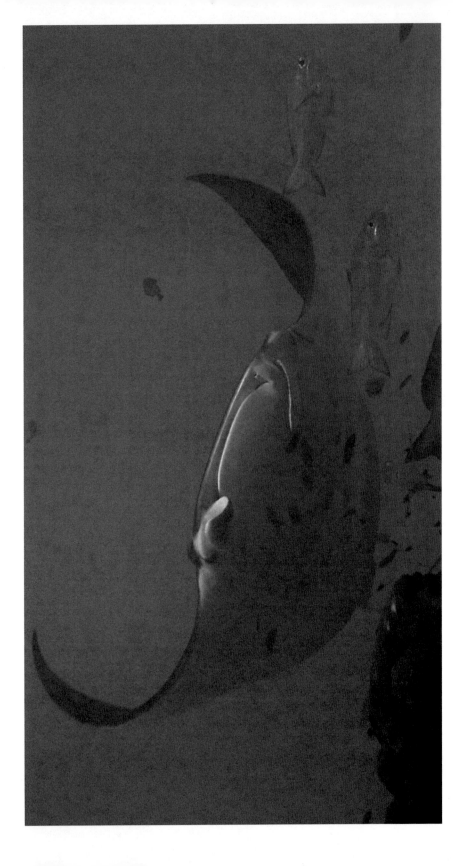

CHARACTERISTICS

Manta Rays are solitary animals and a graceful swimmer. Like other large species of fish, they swim by moving their pectoral fins up and down, which propels their large flat body through the water. Their short tail allows the manta ray to be more acrobatic with movement, and they have even be seen leaping out of the water!

They are known to frequently visit areas of smaller fish where the fish, such as wrasse and angelfish, swim in their gills and over their skin to feed, helping by cleaning the Manta Ray of parasites and dead tissue.

APPEARANCE

Unlike many sharks, Manta Rays do not have teeth and instead pull the food particles out of the water using rows of tiny plates in their mouths. They eat these particles as they swim along.

They are striking in appearance with black and white coloration and enormous size. The manta, unlike other rays, does not have a spine on its tail for defense.

REPRODUCTION

After mating the female lays a couple of eggs, which actually develop and then hatch inside of her body. This process is common in the reproduction of a number of shark and ray species.

Within 6 weeks of hatching, the female manta ray gives birth to 1 or 2 pups, which develop into large adults and go out on their own fairly quickly.

LIFE SPAN

The Manta Ray can live for 15 to 20 years!

SIZE

The Manta Ray is the largest species of ray in the world with wingspan measurements of up to 20 (or even more) feet across. They can weigh as much as 3,000 pounds!

They are VERY BIG!

HABITAT

The Manta Ray is most commonly found in the warm, tropical of waters of the world's oceans, usually around coral reefs and along the continental shelves where there is plenty of food for them to eat. However, because they are so large, they are also commonly spotted hunting out in the open ocean.

DIET

Manta rays eat tiny marine organisms including microscopic plankton, small fish and crustaceans. They eat while they are swimming, by filtering these small aquatic creatures through the plates in their mouths.

ENEMIES

Despite its large size, the relatively docile nature of the Manta Ray means that it is actually preyed upon by a number of large marine predators. Large species of shark such as the great white shark and killer whales are known to hunt and feed on them.

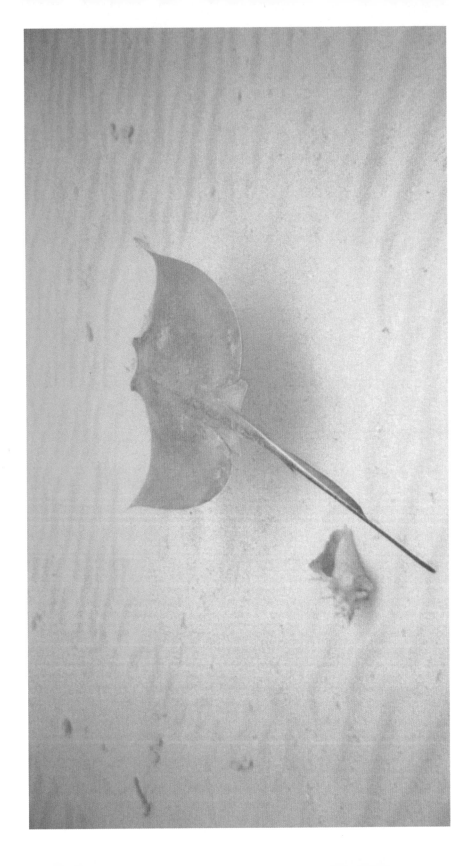

SUITABILITY AS PETS

The Manta Ray is much too big to have as a pet. If you want to visit them, there are aquariums that have a habitat where you can see them swimming and watch them interact with one another.

COLOR ME

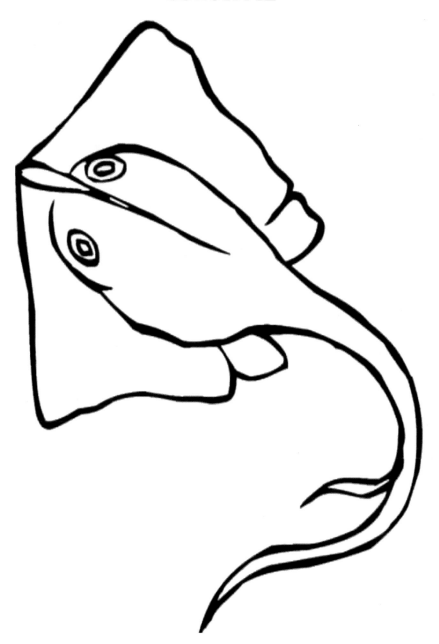

COLOR ME

COLOR ME

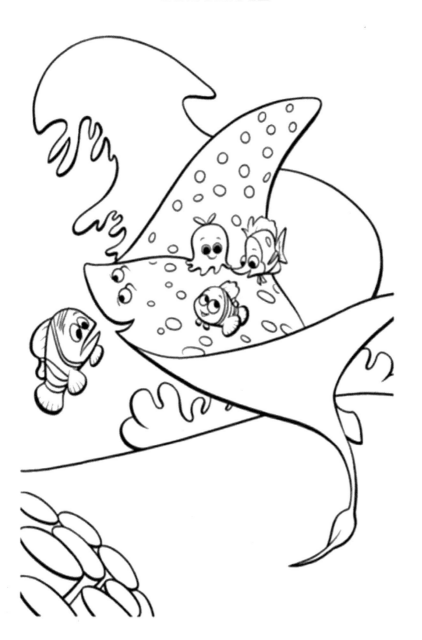

COLOR ME

COLOR ME

COLOR ME

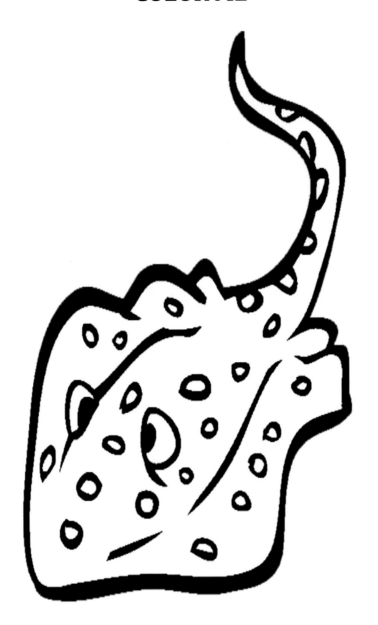

COLOR ME

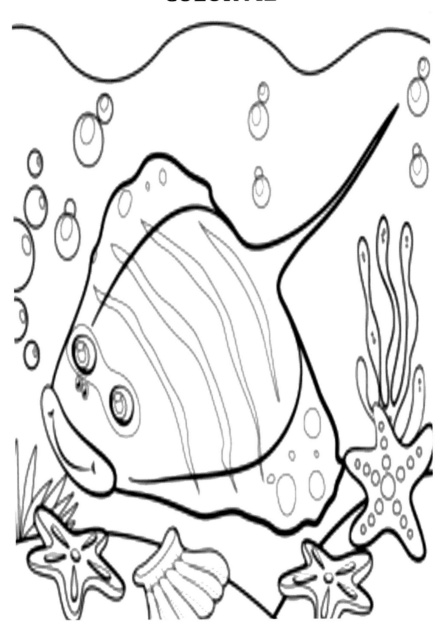

Please leave me a review here:

LisaStrattin.com/Review-Vol-277

For more Kindle Downloads Visit Lisa Strattin Author Page on Amazon Author Central

amazon.com/author/lisastrattin

To see upcoming titles, visit my website at LisaStrattin.com– most books available on Kindle!

LisaStrattin.com

FREE BOOK

FOR ALL SUBSCRIBERS – SIGN UP NOW

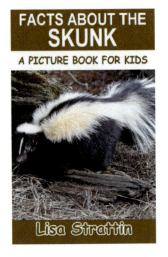

LisaStrattin.com/Subscribe-Here

LisaStrattin.com/Facebook

LisaStrattin.com/Youtube

Made in the USA
Middletown, DE
15 January 2022

58741300R00024